superstars! superstars! superstars! superstars!

CREATIVE EDUCATION SPORTS SUPERSTARS

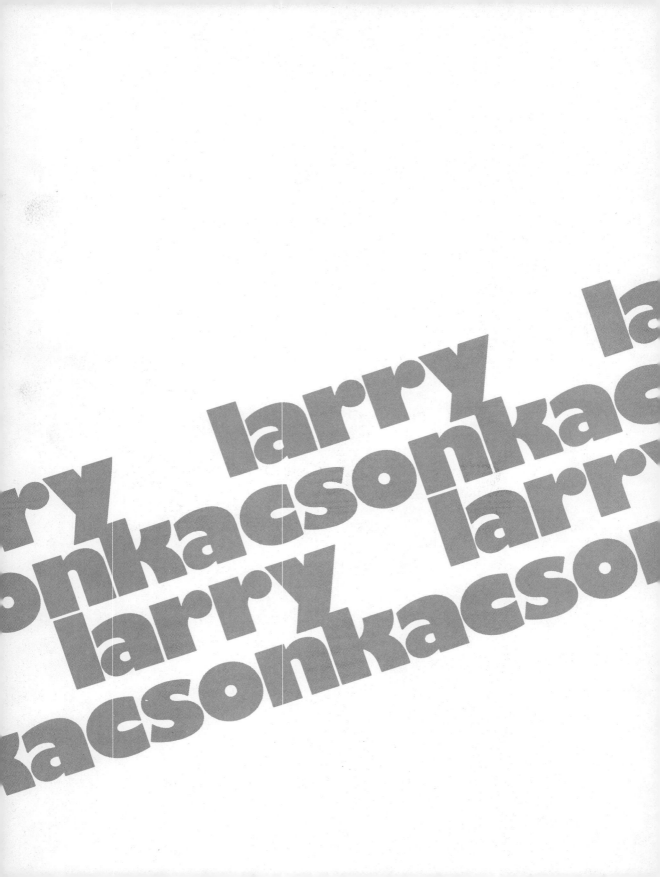

# larry csonka

## by Larry Batson
### illustrated by Harold Henriksen

AMECUS STREET
MANKATO, MINNESOTA

larry

rry

onka

csonka

larry

larry

kacsonka

csonkacsonka

larr

kacso

Published by Amecus Street, 123 South Broad Street, P.O. Box 113,
Mankato, Minnesota 56001

Copyright © 1974 by Amecus Street. International copyrights reserved in all countries.
No part of this book may be reproduced in any form without written permission
from the publisher. Printed in the United States.

Distributed by Childrens Press, 1224 West Van Buren Street, Chicago, Illinois 60607

Library of Congress Numbers: 74-16419     ISBN: 0-87191-382-8

Cover: Photo by Vernon J. Biever

Library of Congress Cataloging in Publication Data
Batson, Larry, 1930-      Larry Csonka.
SUMMARY: Profile of the professional career and attainments of
Larry Csonka, fullback for the Miami Dolphins.
1. Csonka, Larry—Juvenile literature. 2. Football—Biography]
[1. Csonka, Larry. 2. Football—Juvenile literature.
I. Henrikson, Harold, illus.     II. Title.
GV939.C75B37   796.33'2'0924   [B] [92] 74-16419   ISBN 0-87191-382-8

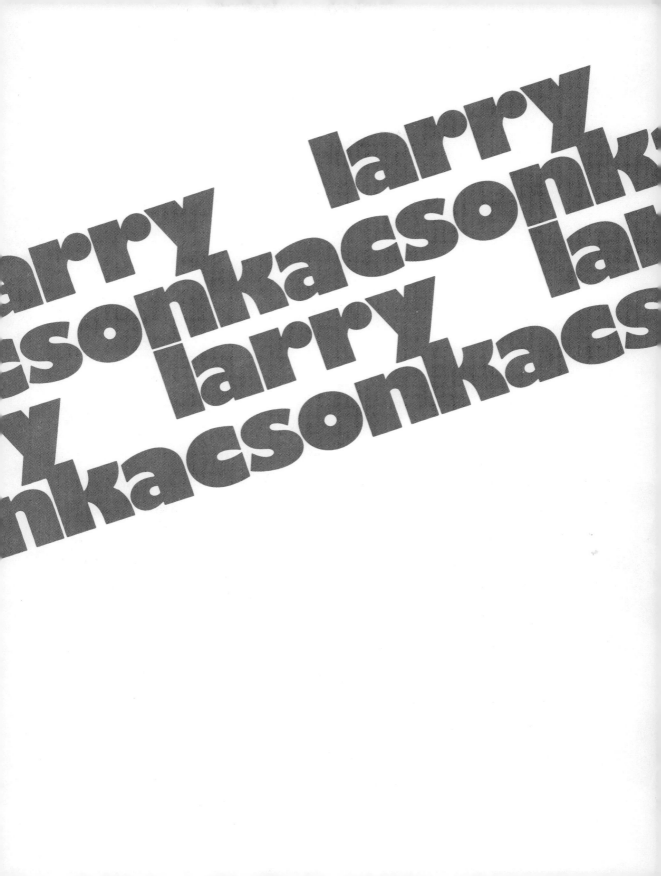

Larry Csonka's favorite football play is a smash through the line. It's a play that matches Csonka's strength and quickness, his power and determination against another team's strongest players and surest tacklers.

"If fans could see and hear what goes on in the middle of the field," Csonka has said, "they'd have a better idea of what football is really like. They'd know what a running back's job is like."

"The noise is tremendous," he said. "The pads and helmets are cracking together; the blockers are grunting when they slam into the defensive players. The defensive players grab and claw at you as you go by. Those guys are huge. Like that old story, they blot out the sun. You run for the daylight between them."

Csonka always insists that his blockers deserve more credit than he does. After his team, the Miami Dolphins, won the 1974 Super Bowl, he said, "What I do around here is no big deal. We have a great offensive line."

Csonka was being modest. His blockers do open holes, but Csonka has the knack of timing and the quickness to hit them at the split-second they open. He has the strength to tear free from the linemen grabbing at him. His power and determination enable him to meet linebackers head-on and carry them for additional yardage.

His strength is awesome. In a college game, he once carried four men on his back for 14 yards. In a professional game against the New York Jets, he put three men who tried to tackle him head-on out of the game. "It was like watching 11 men get run over by a bus," a New York sportswriter wrote.

After the Dolphins defeated the Minnesota Vikings 24-7 in the 1974 Super Bowl, Carl Eller, Minnesota's All-Pro defensive end, talked about Csonka. Eller, one of the strongest men in football, said, "One man can't stop Csonka cold once he gathers momentum. You can't hold him at the line unless you can meet him absolutely straight-on. He'll break any tackle from the side."

Csonka was named most valuable player of that Super Bowl. The 68,000 fans in Rice Stadium at Houston, Texas, stood and cheered him time after time as he scored two touchdowns and set up a third with his smashing runs. Another 80 million fans watched on TV as Csonka carried the ball 33 times and gained 145 yards, both Super Bowl records.

When it was over, Minnesota quarterback Fran Tarkenton said, "I have never seen any fullback play any

better than Csonka did. But that's sort of normal for him."
In the weeks following the Super Bowl, others echoed
Tarkenton's praise. Csonka was acclaimed as the finest
fullback in the game, perhaps the best ever.

But almost no one remembered that if it hadn't been
for his own determination, Csonka would never have been
allowed to play fullback. Nobody recalled that he had been
forced to prove over and over again — in high school, at
Syracuse University, and again with the Dolphins — that
his proper position was fullback, not on the line or at
linebacker.

Csonka saw his first football game when he was nine years old. He decided immediately that he wanted to be a player. He was born on Christmas Day in 1946 at Stow, Ohio, and grew up on a little farm near there. He was baptized Larry Richard, not Lawrence. He was the fourth of six children, three girls and three boys. His brother, Joe, seven years older than Larry, played end on the Stow High School team. When Larry was a third-grader, his father took him one night to watch Joe play.

Joe made a spectacular catch of a pass and Larry's father sent him down to the team bench with a dollar bill as a reward. Larry still remembers standing beside his brother under the lights, the players and coach around him, the crowd yelling in the background. From then on Larry played football every chance he got and waited for the time he could go out for the high school team.

Larry also worked hard on the farm, helping with the livestock and in the garden. One day he set a bucket of water down near a steer. The animal flung up its head and broke Larry's nose. Since then, his nose has been broken nine more times — once while wrestling in high school, four times while playing football in college, and four times with the Dolphins.

Csonka shrugs off injuries like that. He often has

said that he wants to feel sore after a game. It proves that he contributed.

Larry gained 35 pounds and grew three inches the summer before he started eighth grade. He was so big and strong that he was allowed to play with the high school freshman team. He played center on offense and middle guard on defense.

The next year he played on the junior varsity as a defensive end. As a 10th grader he made the varsity team at that position. Late in his 10th grade season, Larry was used on a kick return team to fill in for an injured player. The kick bounced to him and he ran over two tacklers carrying it back.

Wow! It was a great feeling! Larry decided immediately that he was going to be a running back. But he had to convince his coach, and that wasn't easy.

When practice began the next fall, Larry lined up with the backs. His teammates and coaches tried to talk him out of it. "They kept saying, 'You're too big and slow,'" Csonka recalls. "They'd tell me to get back on defense."

Larry refused. He even got into a fight with another player and had to be pulled away by a teammate. That fight convinced the coach that he would have to give Larry a chance to carry the ball. One chance was all it took. He

ran wild in his first game at fullback and played there every game for two seasons.

By the time he finished high school, Larry had reached his full height of 6 feet, 2 inches and weighed 220 pounds — about 20 less than his present playing weight. Although he loved football, he had never really planned on going to college. He was thinking of joining the Merchant Marine.

However, some colleges began writing him. Larry's girl friend, Pam Conley, made him answer the letters. One of them was from Syracuse University in Syracuse, New York. Ben Schwartzwalder was the football coach. He had coached such great running backs as Jim Brown and Jim Nance, both professional stars; the late Ernie Davis, a unanimous All-American; and Floyd Little, then a sophomore at Syracuse and later a star with the Denver Broncos.

Schwartzwalder visited the Csonka farm. "This story is the kind they used to make in the movies," Schwartzwalder said. "As I'm walking up the driveway to the Csonka place, there's a cat and a rabbit fussing on the front lawn. Out the front door comes Larry. He grabs the cat with one hand, the rabbit with the other. I'm telling you this kid's got quickness I can't believe. I gotta have him. . ."

Larry enrolled at Syracuse — and the same old

problem arose. His coaches thought he should play defense.

"To show what a genius I am," Schwartzwalder said later, "I turned Larry into a linebacker. It was the worst mistake I ever made. Our fullback was injured the next year and I moved Larry to the backfield. That was the smartest move I ever made."

Csonka went on to break the rushing records of Brown, Nance, Davis, and Little. He carried the ball 957 times, gained 2,934 yards for an average of 4.9 yards per carry, and was named to most All-American teams. He gained 100 yards or more 14 times. He also became an excellent blocker.

"Larry's senior year," said Schwartzwalder, "we were missing not only Floyd, but also blocking. With him, I could use the term one-man offense without disturbing the morale of the team. In fact, when we showed game films, the boys used to sit there and cheer Larry."

During Csonka's second year at college, he and Pam Conley eloped and were married. Larry moved out of the dormitory where he had been getting free room and board as part of his scholarship. He got a job as a night watchman at a parking lot, working from 8 p.m. to 4 a.m. He had another job, mopping the college gym for $15 a month.

Today when people ask if he got a free ride at college

and secret gifts from alumni, Csonka laughs. He recalls trying to stay awake in classes or practice after working all night.

Larry was a physical education major in college and freely admits that many of his courses were easy ones. But he took some hard ones, like business administration, and a lot of English literature, his favorite subject. He is about a semester short of credits for a degree. "I wish I had that degree," he has said. "I've been lucky in football but if I had been injured, I'd have needed the degree."

In 1968 Larry was the first choice of the Miami Dolphins in the annual National Football League draft. He had barely heard of the team but was happy to be going to a warm climate. That summer at the College All-Star Game in Chicago, he met another Dolphin draft choice. Jim Kiick was a carefree running back from New Jersey and the University of Wyoming. Csonka and Kiick liked each other immediately. They later earned fame on the playing field as "Butch Cassidy and the Sundance Kid." They remained the closest of friends even though Csonka became one of the game's great stars while Kiick became a substitute.

Despite Csonka's great college record, many people in professional football predicted that he would never be-

come an outstanding professional fullback. "Too big and too slow. He should switch to linebacker or defensive end," they said. It was the same criticism Csonka had heard in high school and college.

For two years it appeared that the critics at last might be right. Csonka rushed for 540 yards in 1968 and 566 in 1969. Those were just average results for a team that was

poorer than average. The Dolphins won just five games in 1968 and only three the next year.

Then in 1970 Don Shula came to Miami as head coach. Shula is noted for his brilliant football mind and his willingness to work hard himself and to drive his team to the point of exhaustion in training camp. An emotional man who loves to laugh, Shula also has a hot temper. "He's another crazy Hungarian like my father," said Csonka. Later the big fullback said many times, "Shula's the best coach in football."

Shula ordered four full-scale workouts a day at his first Miami camp. Two is customary in pro football and one is usually without pads. The Dolphins didn't know what to make of Shula, but they were too busy to complain. The fourth daily workout began at 7 p.m. and often lasted until after dark.

Csonka tells this story of one of them: "One night I lined up to run a pass play and from about 40 yards away in the dark, Shula barked at me, 'Csonka, what the heck are you doing?' I didn't know what I'd done. Then he said, 'You're lined up a step too wide. If a linebacker blitzed, you couldn't block him.' Boy! Right then I knew I had to concentrate every second with him around."

The two Hungarians, Csonka and Shula, became friends. They argued often but respected each other. And Csonka worked hard in practice. When he disagreed with an order or wanted an explanation, he asked Shula in private.

Shula has admitted that when he came to Miami he was doubtful of Csonka's ability. But as he watched Dolphin game films hour after hour, Shula changed his mind.

The first thing coaches notice about Csonka is the quickness with which he gets under way. They call this attribute "quick feet," and for an inside runner it is more important than actual speed.

The second impressive thing about Csonka is his strength. He has massive thighs that can drive right through the arms of defensive linemen. His forearms are huge and he uses them as clubs. He can slow a charging linebacker with a forearm smash or bowl over a smaller defensive back.

Csonka is a ferocious runner, an attacker. He seems to love contact. Once in a game against the Buffalo Bills, he was so eager to get past a defender that he reached out and smashed him to the ground with his fist. It may have been the only time in National Football League history that a ball carrier was charged with a personal foul.

Csonka is not a fancy runner. His nickname "Zonk" is a good description of his style. He doesn't fake or move around much. He makes one adjustment as he starts his rush — he lines himself up with the hole. Once he is through the line, he turns straight upfield.

He doesn't try to run around tacklers. He hits them. Like most good running backs, Csonka keeps his feet close to the ground, making him very hard to knock off balance. He takes long steps and tries to hit tacklers when he's halfway through a step with one foot off the ground. That lessens chances of injury. Most knee injuries happen when a player's foot is firmly planted. Csonka's weight, strength, and powerful legs sometimes enable him to carry tacklers for several yards.

Csonka averages about five yards a carry. That is the key to the Miami offense. The Dolphins can control the ball. Then when the opponent masses to stop Csonka,

a pass or an end run often catches them off balance.

Csonka's runs look like simple plays, but they aren't. They require precise timing and coordination because of two things. First, defensive players change their positions frequently before the ball is snapped. Blockers have to hit them where they are, not where they would like them to be. This means that the hole for the runner may open at any of several spots. Second, the blockers can hold off the defensive linemen only for an instant. Most of the time, the hole opens and closes quickly.

Csonka speaks of "running to daylight." Actually, what he must do is anticipate where the hold is going to be and then time his rush to hit it at the proper split-second. Csonka is a master at this. The offensive linemen at Miami greatly appreciate it. After all, if the ball carrier picks the wrong spot to run or gets there too soon or too late, the linemen's work is wasted.

When Csonka does make a mistake, his blockers often kid him in the huddle. Against Oakland in the final play-off game before the 1974 Super Bowl, Zonk ran the wrong way and was clobbered. Three or four teammates started yelling at him. "Nag, nag, nag," growled Zonk, who then took the ball 11 yards for a touchdown on the next play. He scored two more that day, a play-off record. "They didn't have to yell at me," he said later, laughing at the memory. "That Oakland end nearly tore my head off."

The Dolphins are serious about winning but also know that the game can produce some laughs. Csonka and his buddy, Kiick, often play the leading roles in the club's humor department.

The movie "Butch Cassidy and the Sundance Kid" was a hit in 1969 when the Dolphins won 10 games with the two pals starring in the backfield. The movie characters seemed to fit. Kiick became "Butch Cassidy" and Csonka "Sundance." Both players saw the film several times and sometimes swapped lines from it during the game.

Once at Los Angeles, half a dozen Rams players piled on Kiick as he tried an end sweep. He got up slowly and said to Csonka, "Who are those guys, Kid? We ain't comin' back this way."

"Games are fun," Csonka has said. "It's the practices they have to pay me for."

Nevertheless, Csonka works hard in practice, earning the respect of his coaches. "Csonka is the complete fullback — running, blocking, and catching passes," says Miami assistant coach Carl Taseff. "Larry knows his assignments so well that he doesn't have to think what he's going to do, just react. And he'll play when he's hurt."

Coaches and players know that physical ability alone is not enough to carry an athlete to stardom. It takes mental toughness, determination, the will power to force yourself to go as hard as you can and as far as you can on every play of every game. Csonka has that mental drive. He demonstrated it in one of professional football's most famous games, a double-overtime game for the division championship at Kansas City on Christmas Day of 1971.

The regular game ended in a 24-24 tie as the Dolphins came from behind three times to tie the score. Since it was a play-off game, the rules provided that it continue with a sudden death overtime. The first team to score would win.

Neither team scored in the first 15-minute overtime. The second one was about half over when Miami quarterback Bob Griese called one of Csonka's favorite plays, one which hadn't been used that day. Kiick would fake a sweep to the right. Csonka, the ball carrier, would take one step in that direction before cutting back through the left side of the line. Starting from the Miami 35-yard line, Csonka ran 29 yards to the Kansas City 36. It was close enough for Garo Yepremian to kick a field goal and give Miami a 27-24 victory in the longest football game in history.

Most of the Dolphins were jumping around the

locker room, yelling happily after the game. Not Csonka. He was so tired he could barely stand. He had lost 15 pounds during the game.

The Dolphins went on from that game to the American Conference championship and the 1972 Super Bowl which they lost 24-3 to Dallas.

The next season they were unbeaten in 17 straight games, including a 14-7 win over the Washington Redskins in the 1973 Super Bowl. When Miami went to the Super Bowl again in 1974, they became the first team to go three straight times.

Those seasons were years of stardom for Csonka, too. He gained 1,051 yards in 1971, the first time he had gone over 1,000. In 1972 he gained 1,117 yards and in 1973 he had 1,003.

But while the "Sundance Kid" was riding high, his buddy "Butch Cassidy" wasn't doing so well. Jim Kiick was replaced in the Dolphins' backfield by Mercury Morris, a swifter and more elusive runner.

Kiick was unhappy at losing his starting job. Csonka, his best friend, was also sorry to see it happen. But he didn't take it out on Morris.

"Csonka was the key," said Coach Shula. "He could have destroyed our unity by taking sides, but he accepted Mercury. Seeing that, Kiick did too.

Except for Kiick, Csonka doesn't see much of the Dolphin players off the field. He and his wife, Pam, and their two sons, Doug and Paul, live in a pleasant neighborhood in Plantation, Florida, a suburb of Miami. Their closest friends are not in football.

Csonka has become one of the most sought-after speakers in the country. His fee for an appearance is $2,000 plus expenses, yet he gets 10 times as many invitations as he can accept.

As a speaker, he is just like he is in private conversation — pleasant, courteous, and humorous. He likes to joke and to laugh at other people's stories. He is interested in many subjects and he is a good listener. People sometimes express surprise that he can speak so well. That upsets Csonka a little bit.

"Just because you see me butt heads and go off tackle for four yards," he said once, "that doesn't mean I go around with my hands scraping the ground, eat raw meat, have fangs, and live in a dark room under the stadium. I'm not big and dumb. I enjoy talking to groups. I've got a little ham in me and when I get out of football, I want to go into acting or radio or TV work."

One topic Csonka usually touches on in his talks is the overemphasis on football he sees at the grade school level.

"I'm talking about kids between the ages of 6 and 11," he said. "They've got uniforms and frustrated Vince Lombardis for coaches. And it's a battle to make the play-offs and this and that. Win, win, win, that's what the kids are hearing when they are six and seven. Well, how would you like to be seven years old and sitting on the bench because you are third string? Imagine the feeling of inadequacy that kid must face.

"I can accept Don Shula hollering at me on a particular play. But I don't want some guy doing it to my seven-year-old boy. At that age the kids should be playing

flag football or touch, whatever you want to call it. Dress 'em up in equipment, that's fine. But don't start counting down to the Super Bowl. Let them have some fun."

Csonka loves fishing and camping. He used to be an avid hunter, but in recent years he stopped that. He now goes to the wilderness to look at animals, not to kill them.

He talks often of his boyhood and how he and his brother slept in an unfinished attic room that was "so cold I could watch my breath go the length of the room. I had a runny nose the first 10 years of my life."

Csonka's mother says Larry was "ornery but never mean" and always on the go. He was so insistent on following his older brother Joe around that Joe would sometimes tie him to a tree or put rocks in his diapers to slow him down.

All of the Csonka children worked hard. "I hated that farm until I was old enough to know better," Csonka said once. "Now I think how rewarding it was — growing things, having animals. Hey, there was a creek and about 20 dogs running around. And we chased woodchucks and climbed trees to get baby crows for pets.

"Think how ironic it is. My dad didn't have much money and here I am with two boys who are rich kids by comparison. Yet I'm trying to get enough to afford to give them the life my dad gave me."

Csonka's salary with the Dolphins as they went to three straight Super Bowls was $60,000 a year. But he won't have to worry about financial security any longer.

In March of 1974, Csonka, Jim Kiick, and Paul Warfield, a star pass receiver for the Dolphins, signed contracts to play in the new World Football League. The total was reported to be $3 million. It was said that Csonka would be paid $500,000 a year during the three-year contract.

The contract starts in 1975 after Csonka plays one final year with Miami but the money has been guaranteed.

The three Miami Stars had signed with a Toronto team in the World Football League. Before the new league began its first season in July 1974, the Toronto franchise was in Memphis, Tennessee. While the Memphis Southmen played their 20-game 1974 schedule, Larry Csonka remained a Dolphin.

"I love football; I loved playing for the Dolphins and Don Shula is the best coach in football," Csonka had said after signing with the new league. "I'm going to do my best to help the Dolphins win again."

Csonka would like nothing better than to finish his stay in Miami by leading the Dolphins to a fourth-straight Super Bowl.

JACK NICKLAUS
BILL RUSSELL
MARK SPITZ
VINCE LOMBARDI
BILLIE JEAN KING
ROBERTO CLEMENTE
JOE NAMATH
BOBBY HULL
HANK AARON
JERRY WEST
TOM SEAVER
JACKIE ROBINSON
MUHAMMAD ALI
O. J. SIMPSON
JOHNNY BENCH
WILT CHAMBERLAIN
ARNOLD PALMER
A. J. FOYT
JOHNNY UNITAS
GORDIE HOWE

# superstars!
# superstars!
# superstars!
# superstars

CREATIVE EDUCATION SPORTS SUPERSTARS

WALT FRAZIER
PHIL AND TONY ESPOSITO
BOB GRIESE
FRANK ROBINSON
PANCHO GONZALES
LEE TREVINO
KAREEM ABDUL JABBAR
JEAN CLAUDE KILLY
EVONNE GOOLAGONG
ARTHUR ASHE
SECRETARIAT
ROGER STAUBACH
FRAN TARKENTON
BOBBY ORR
LARRY CSONKA
BILL WALTON
ALAN PAGE
PEGGY FLEMING
OLGA KORBUT
DON SCHULA
MICKEY MANTLE
EVEL KNIEVEL